God's little book of Prayer

Richard Daly

First published 2002
Copyright © 2002

All rights reserved. No part of this publication
may be reproduced in any form without prior
permission from the publisher.

British Library Cataloguing in Publication Data.
A catalogue record for this book is available
from the British Library.

ISBN 1-903921-03-1

Printed and published by
Autumn House Limited
Grantham, Lincs.

Introduction

This is a little book dealing with a huge theme. Yet in these pages lie small nuggets of spiritual truth designed to challenge and encourage you to keep prayer at the top of your spiritual agenda.

Open this book at any page and take a moment just to reflect on the words. Use the scriptural reference at the bottom of each passage to gain a deeper insight.

May you be truly enriched.

Richard Daly

God Cares

God is interested in your prayers
because He is interested in you.
Whatever matters to you,
matters to God.

Zeph. 3:17

Expect the Unexpected

When you pray,
God responds.
Difficult situations change.
Unexplained miracles occur.
Unexpected events take place.

Jer. 33:3; John 14:13, 14

Just say it

In prayer
there is no need
to rehearse a speech.
Simply voice your feelings.
He will assure you:
'I know how you feel.'

Psalm 139:1, 2

Pray with passion

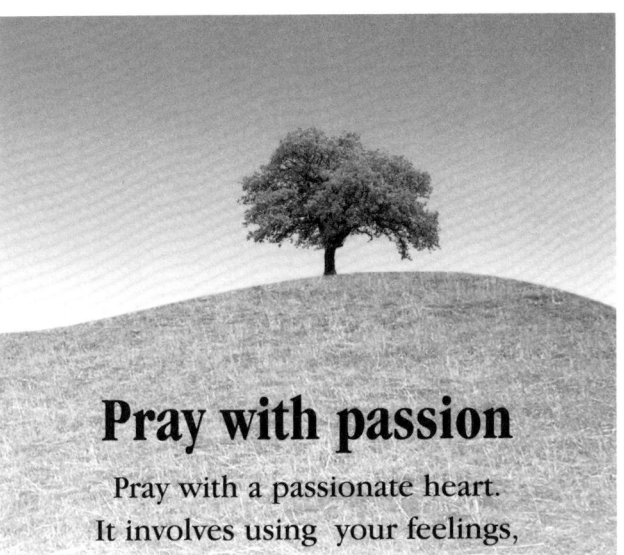

Pray with a passionate heart.
It involves using your feelings,
thoughts and imagination,
to open yourself to the divine
presence in your soul.

Luke 10:27

Be silent!

Open yourself to the depths of God's love. Simply be still in His presence of love. No words are necessary.

Zech. 2:13; Psalm 46:10

Be happy

Let laughter set your spirit free.
Let it relax, release and heal you.

Prov. 17:22; John 15:11

Off load

Don't be afraid to tell God
how angry you feel.
He can handle it!

Deut. 26:7

Inhale God's love

Be quiet. Relax. Breathe in deeply
the boundless love of God.
Breathe out anxiety and fear,
breathe in divine peace . . .
out tensions and worry.

1 Peter 5:7

God is already there

Remember! God is already in the
future of our lives; He's at work
without our even knowing it.

Isa. 65:24

Seek God's compassion

The Scriptures are full of
comforting words:
'Do not be afraid,'
'Do not be anxious!'
'Be at peace',
'Trust God'.
Don't you think there must
be a reason for these
repeated admonitions?

Prov. 18:10

Recall God's mercies

Reflect on the joys in your life.
Thank God for His blessings.

Deut. 9:7; Ps. 103:2

Let God lead

Don't ask God to bless
your plans. Ask Him to show
you His. They are already blessed!

Psalm 33:11

Be assured

God will never tell you to do anything that doesn't line up with what He has already told you in His Word.

Prov. 2:6

Wait

If it isn't God's timing ... wait!
At the right time, the plan
will be clear. The right person
will show up, funds will be
provided, the door will
be opened.
Trust Him!

Eccles. 3:1

Stay in touch

Your prayers can be verbal or silent,
long or short, public or private,
the idea is to be in conscious
contact with God at all times.

1 Thess. 5:17

Experience true intimacy

The most intimate
communion with God
comes only through prayer.

1 John 4:16

Sing a prayer

In prayer try singing praises to God instead of speaking them. Allow the melody to flow from your heart. Don't be concerned if your voice sounds somewhat unpleasant!

Psalm 135:3

Seek God's power

God is capable of handling any situation. Creating planets isn't much of a problem. Neither is raising the dead. Nothing is too hard, but He's waiting for you to recognise His power and ask for help.

Gen. 18:14

Prayer changes things

Prayer changes you!

John 14:13, 14

Be sincere

Simply talk to God as a friend,
sincerely and personally.
There's no need for fancy phrases.

Prov. 18:24

Keep going

Is a difficulty immobilising you?
Prayer can get you moving.

Matt. 17:19, 20

Examine yourself

Sometimes our own sins can block answers to prayer. Let the prayer of the psalmist be one of yours: Search me, O God, and know my thoughts; See if there be some wicked way in me. Cleanse me from every sin, and set me free.

Psalm 139

He's able

Through prayer the impossibilities
of man become the possibilities of God.

Matt. 10:27

Take your time

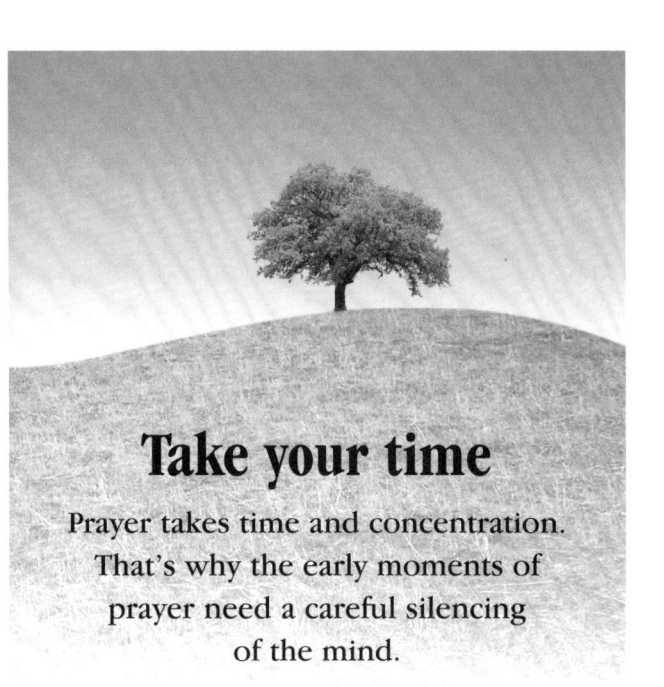

Prayer takes time and concentration.
That's why the early moments of
prayer need a careful silencing
of the mind.

Isaiah 41:1

Be true

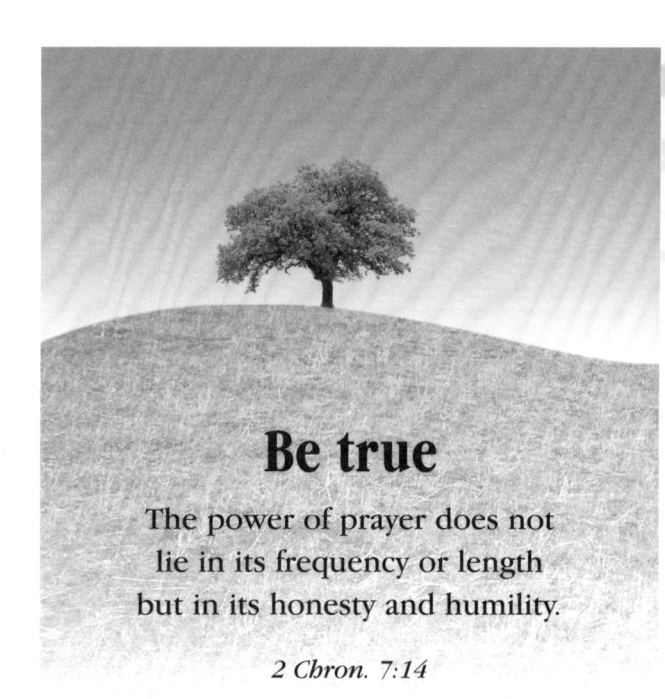

The power of prayer does not
lie in its frequency or length
but in its honesty and humility.

2 Chron. 7:14

Be holy

Holy living promotes
holy praying.

1 Peter 1:15

Prove God

Prayer in the hand of faith
commissions the armies
of God to action!

Psalm 91:15

Seek forgiveness

The prayer that God will always answer immediately is the prayer of sincere repentance.

Psalm 34:18

Thought transplant

In the presence of God,
prayer enables you to replace
your thoughts with His.

Phil. 2:5

Be consistent

Seven days without prayer
makes one weak!

1 Chron. 29:10-13

Make prayer sacrificial

Pray even when you don't feel like it. It may involve a sacrifice that goes beyond your normal routine – but the results are infinitely rewarding.

Rom. 12:11

Experience oneness

Intimacy… what a word picture
describing two becoming one.
Yet this is exactly what happens
when you pray. Your spirit unites
with the Spirit of God.

Phil. 2:1-2

Avoid procrastination

When prayer is neglected,
the frequent result is the familiar
feeling of being overwhelmed,
over-run, beaten down, pushed
around and defeated. Don't let
it happen to you!

Psalm 42:11

Live in Him

Jesus gives us the blueprint
for answered prayer in just
one verse: 'If you abide in me,
and my words abide in you,
you will ask what you desire,
and it shall be done for you.'
The secret is living in Him.

John 15:7

Praise means prizes

The full meaning of praise can
be found in its old French origin:
preiser, which means 'to prize'.
Prize means to value,
esteem and cherish.
Think what this means
when we praise God.

Psalm 148

He can do it!

One of the qualities of God
is that He is immutable.
He does not change. Hence His mighty
acts that were performed for
others in the Bible. He is more than
capable of doing for you today
what He did in Bible times.

Heb. 13:8; Mal. 3:6

Pray for something definite

In prayer, focus on
something definite.
Don't let the mind wander.
All effectual prayers recorded
in the Bible are those that
focused on one thing.

James 5:13-15

Yield

Praying effectively involves yielding to God; being in acquiescence to His revealed will.

James 4:7

Pray with worthy desire

Jacob exclaimed in an agony of desire,
'I will not let you go unless you bless me.'
Was God displeased with his boldness
and importunity? Not at all!

Gen. 32:26

Pray with right motives

After prayer, take time to examine the petitions that you have made. Were your motives, though seemingly good, rooted in selfishness – or in supreme regard for the glory of God?

2 Thess. 1:12

Renounce sins

Effective prayer comes with renouncing sins; not only acknowledging and repenting of them, but purposing in your heart to give them up for ever.

Psalm 51

Pray in faith

Don't look for an answer to prayer if you pray without expecting to obtain one.

2 Corinthians 1:11

Seek God's rest

You will know if you have truly cast your burdens at the feet of Jesus. Your soul will find peaceful rest, with an inexpressible and glorious joy.

1 Peter 1:8

Please God

One of the most pleasing prayers to God is the one that, with perseverance, asks for the conversion of a soul.

Luke 15:7

Keep in tune

Knowing the right thing to ask
for in prayer will not be a problem
to the person whose life is united
with Christ. It will come naturally.

Matt. 21:22

Claim His promises

In whatever circumstance
you may be placed, God has
provided in the Bible some
promise, either general or
specific, which you can claim,
that is precisely suited to
your case.

2 Cor. 1:20

Submit

Entire submission to God is indispensable to the prayer of faith. Your time, talents, influence – all you are, all you have – are to be His entirely.

Job 22:21

Be Holy-Spirit driven

The Spirit of God leads
individual Christians to pray
for things that they would not
normally pray for unless
they were led by the Spirit.

Psalm 73:21-24

Power prayer

Prayer is power:
a power and strength
that influences God.

Psalm 68:34, 35

Be watchful

People sometimes pray but never pay attention to see if the prayer is granted. You must watch in prayer!

Matt. 26:41

Trust and obey

When God commands us
to do something, it is the
best possible evidence
that we can do it.

Phil. 4:13

Receive God's provisions

God is ready to fill your empty
hands as you would never believe;
if only you will lift them up to Him
in obedience and trust.

Isaiah 46:11

Accept God's offer

God offers special grace to
match every shade of sorrow.

2 Cor. 12:9

Endure

The word endure means
'to bear up under a load.'
This patient bearing of life's
cumbersome loads is made
possible by prayer.

1 Peter 2:20

Be blessed

There is something about
suffering that simplifies life
and draws us back to the basics.

Matt. 5:10-12

Accept God's way

When God says 'no', it is not
a sign of rejection, but
simply redirection.

Prov. 3:5, 6

Rejoice through trials

If you're going through a trial right now that has forced you to your knees. Maybe it's drawing you closer to the Lord than you've ever been before. For such a thing give thanks.

Psalm 71:20

Seek God's way

Through prayer, God does
not offer temporary relief.
He offers a permanent solution.

Psalm 18:2

Be resilient

We can face whatever life throws at us when, through prayer, our strength is sourced in God.

2 Cor. 12:10

Go forward

In answer to prayer, sometimes
God gives us just enough light
so that we can take the next step.
In reality, that's all we need.

Isaiah 30:21

Discipline yourself

To trust God completely is
to take Him at His word. That
requires the discipline of surrender.

Psalm 146

Let go

Our problem is that we hold
on to our problems. In prayer,
let go and let God.

John 16:33

Do first things first

Remember the golden rule
of prayer: 'Seek first the
righteousness of God ...
and all the other things will
be added to you.'

Matt. 6:33

Trust Him

God always knows
what He is doing.

Isaiah 55:7-9

Seek God's shelter

When times are tough, the Lord is our only security. In times of darkness He is our Light; in times of weakness the Lord is our only strength.

Psalm 34:19

Return a gift of time

Consider giving God a daily gift of time. Not just a few spare minutes here and there, but a substantial gift. It would be time well spent alone with God.

Psalm 55:17

Act!

Prayer does not require advanced education. Only an act of the will is needed.

Isaiah 58:9

More prayer, more power

Where there is an absence of prayer there will be an absence of power. Where there is frequency of prayer there will be a continual display of God's power.

Jer. 33:3

Pray!

For a Christian prayer is not
a mere option. On the contrary,
it is imperative!

Mark 14:38

Home truths

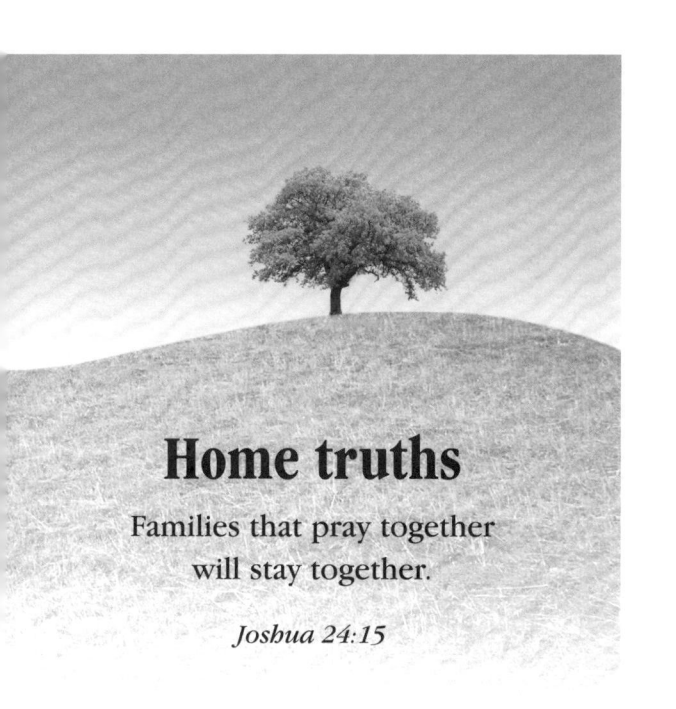

Families that pray together
will stay together.

Joshua 24:15

Take the direct line

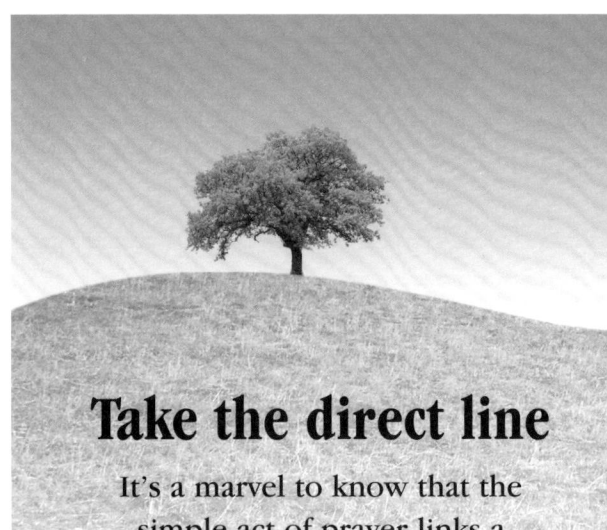

It's a marvel to know that the simple act of prayer links a Sovereign God to finite man.

Jer. 29:12

Get in line

Through prayer you align
yourself to the purpose and will
of God and He is able to do through
you things which He could not
do otherwise.

Psalm 145:18, 19

Be steadfast

Consistency in prayer is the evidence of a consistent relationship.

Daniel 6:10

Use time wisely

What we are depends on
what we receive from the Lord.
What we receive is proportional
to the time spent alone in prayer.

Luke 6:38

Claim the victory

Be prepared! Once we
determine that prayer is important,
our spiritual battles begin. But
be comforted: the battle
is not ours!

1 Sam. 17:47

Seek Him

Carefully mark this on your mind:
It is possible to make time for prayer.

Jer. 29:13

Be doers!

Only when we apply our knowledge of prayer to the actual practice of prayer will we discover the real power of prayer.

James 1:22

Praise Him!

Praise puts God in His rightful position at the very outset of our praying. Through praise we declare His sovereignty and matchless power.

Psalm 22:3

Avoid the obstacles

Until known sin is fully dealt
with we are not ready to pray.

Psalm 66:18

Be quiet!

Being silent in prayer allows
us to think of no thought other
than the Father, Son and Holy Spirit.

Zech. 2:13

Cleanse the soul

The New Testament Greek word for 'confess' means, 'to agree with God' concerning His opinion on a matter. No wonder confession is good for the soul!

James 5:16

Be faithful in little things

During your time of confession, bring before God those daily, sinful habits that can grow to cause severe damage.

Prov. 28:13

Pray with the Scriptures

The Scriptures are rich in
material to feed and stimulate.
As you read them, turn them
into prayer. Bring God's Word
alive in your prayers.

1 Thess. 2:13

Tell Him all

Jesus invites you to share
your worries and troubles.
He says, 'Come unto me . . .
and I will give you rest.'

Matt. 11:28, 29

Be a visionary

Vision is the art of seeing things invisible. To 'watch' in prayer is to open our spiritual eyes to perceive the invisible secrets of God.

Col. 4:2

Win! Win!

In your time of trial, through prayer, God can either move the obstacle or give you the strength to go through it. Either way you win!

Psalm 55:22

Be a co-labourer

Through intercessory prayer we become fully involved with God's work – the redemption of another soul.

Rom.1:9, 10

Just ask

Some things God will not give until we want them enough to ask.

Matt. 7:7

Pray the Jabez prayer

We must not hesitate to pray as
Jabez prayed, 'Bless me, indeed.'

1 Chron. 4:9, 10.

Be specific

A petition should be specific. It shouldn't be so vague that, within minutes of your prayer, you have forgotten what you've prayed for. If so, perhaps you really didn't need it!

1 John 5:14, 15

Lift Him up!

God is greatly pleased when we come before Him with petitions that will honour His name.

John 12:27, 28

Give thanks

Thanksgiving in prayer helps us focus on what God has done specifically for us. Take time, therefore, to return thanks specifically.

Phil. 4:6

Pray in song

No fewer than forty-one of the Psalms specifically refer to 'singing praises' to the Lord. Surely there must be joy in giving a personal 'song offering' to the Lord in prayer.

Psalm 100

Claim it back!

Through prayer you have the authority to take from the enemy everything he has taken from you.

Job 42:10-12

Meditate on God's Word

There are over thirty thousand promises in Scripture. Each promise is a focus for meditation.

Isaiah 26:3

Count your blessings

In times of discouragement
and distress . . . look back to the
many blessings God has given you
in recent days. Let these thoughts
soothe your anxieties.

Psalm 143:5

Stop, look and listen

In the midst of prayer, stop and just listen! You will absorb divine instructions from God concerning particular matters for that day.

Isaiah 30:21

Learn the secret of friendship

Best friends are always good listeners.
If we truly desire to be friends with God,
we must learn the secret of listening in
God's university of silence.

1 Thess. 4:11, 12

Discover God's will

We do not engage in prayer just to tell God what we want to do. The goal is to discover what God wants us to do.

Psalm 25:4, 5

Tune in to God

God alone knows the solution
to every problem we will face.
Listening in prayer allows us to
tune in to God's solutions.

Eccles. 5:1, 2

Take notes

Next time you pray, why not come equipped with pen and paper? It says to God, 'I believe You will truly speak to me, and I have come prepared to record Your instructions'.

Hab. 2:2, 3

Pray to glorify

The fundamental purpose of prayer is the glorifying of God.

John 13:31, 32

Live prayerfully

Perhaps the greatest challenge to a prayerful life is to adopt and maintain an ongoing prayerful attitude after prayer has ended.

Matt. 5:43-48

Prayer works

There is much we can do after we have prayed, but nothing we can do until we have prayed.

John 15:5

Stand on the promise

When you stand on a
promise of God, and stand on
it unwaveringly . . . that promise
will carry you through.

Joshua 21:45

Pray for God's will

Knowing God's will is always
a dilemma for the Christian.
But being 'filled with the Spirit'
enables you to be in tune with the
thoughts of God. Ask God's
Spirit to fill you today.

Eph. 5:16-18

Hold on

When you are burdened with a
load of care, look up ... reach up
and get a hold of the hand of God,
and don't let go until He blesses you.

Job 12:10

Test your patience

Delays in answers to prayer are for our own benefit. They are our chance to see whether our faith is constant and sincere, or changeable like the waves of the sea.

Psalm 27:13, 14

Parents keep praying

One of the greatest joys as a
parent is praying for your children.
Even if, in their adulthood, they
travel on a 'wayward path',
never give up!

Isaiah 49:25; Prov. 22:6

Don't be deceived

The devil will do anything and everything to keep us from time spent in prayer: television, overwork, tiredness . . . the list is endless. Why do you think he tries so hard? What is it that he knows about the power of prayer?

James 2:19

Set an example

We know little children love
to imitate. What an influence,
therefore, when a child catches
his parents kneeling in the
act of prayer!

Luke 18:15-17

Be confident in Him

God never asks you to do
anything He does not
prepare you to do.

Judges 6:14-16

Let the Holy-Spirit lead

Always remember that true
prayer is Holy Spirit inspired.
That is, the Holy Spirit puts God's
desires into our hearts, and then
we put them into words.

Rom. 8:26

Try praying aloud

Praying aloud helps you focus on what you're saying. This reinforces your thinking and enables you to concentrate on the words.

Psalm 55:16, 17

Claim your doctorate

You may not be privileged to graduate with a PhD, but in the School of Prayer you can achieve it when you **Pray harder Daily**.

Matt. 6:6-13

Stand strong

The devil is no match for even the weakest sinner who humbles himself before God in prayer.

James 4:7

Be spiritually-minded

Your most cherished thoughts
make you what you are.

Prov. 23:17, 18

Move mountains

Jesus said that the prayer of
faith can move mountains.
This faith comes not by looking
at the mountain but by looking
at the Mountain-Mover.

Matt. 17:20; Zech. 4:6

Walk in faith

If you want to walk on water,
you've got to get out of the boat!

Matt. 14:26-29

Be Spirit-led

Let your feelings of inadequacy drive you to God. You will find your adequacy in Him.

James 4:8-10

Endure hardship

God uses growth through
pain to make our faith
more effective.

2 Tim. 2:3

Live prayerfully

One true test of our sincerity
and fervency in prayer is whether
we continue with that state of
mind after prayer.

2 Tim. 1:13, 14

Set the right goals

Our goal ought not to be
self-confidence but Christ-confidence.

Prov. 3:5, 6

Stand tall

A lot of kneeling keeps one
in good standing.

Eph. 3:14-16

Amen and amen!

The word 'Amen' means 'so be it' or 'it is done'. When we close our prayers in this way we are inadvertently agreeing with God's will: 'Let it be done.'

Rev. 22:20, 21